Weird
Kitchen Creations
Chemistry

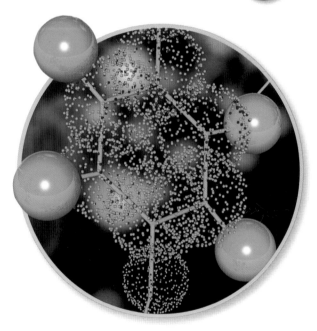

By Molly F. Wetterschneider

Wright
Group

Weird Chemistry: Kitchen Creations
Copyright © 2005 Wright Group/McGraw-Hill
Text by Molly F. Wetterschneider

Explore More™ is a trademark of the McGraw-Hill Companies, Inc.

Wright Group/McGraw-Hill
1 Prudential Plaza
130 E. Randolph
Suite 400 Chicago, IL 60601
www.WrightGroup.com

Printed in the United States

ISBN: 1-4045-2829-6
ISBN: 1-4045-2877-6 (6-pack)

1 2 3 4 5 6 7 8 9 PBM 10 09 08 07 06 05 04

Contents

Introduction

"When we decode a cookbook, every one of us is a practicing chemist. Cooking is really the oldest, most basic application of physical and chemical forces to natural materials."

—Chemist Arthur E. Grosser of McGill University

You may think of **chemists** as people who work in laboratories full of beakers, tubes, and jars. That's often true, but did you know that you can be a chemist, too? In fact, you are already a chemist if you've ever wondered about such things as why food looks different after you cook it or why water turns into ice in the freezer. Being a chemist means looking carefully at things in the world and asking questions about why they are the way they are.

In this book, you will read about the **chemistry** of everyday things. You will also get a chance to use chemistry to do a lot of weird things!

Safety goggles are one of the most important pieces of equipment to have when performing chemistry experiments.

The activities in this book use common household products. These products are highlighted in color in the text so you can easily see what supplies you need to do the activities. Remember to follow these six simple safety rules to avoid getting hurt.

- Always have an adult nearby when you perform any chemistry activity.

- Ask for help if you spill or break something.

- Wear goggles, gloves, and an apron when working with toxic chemicals.

- Get permission from an adult before you use any materials not suggested in the activity.

- Always wash your hands after doing a chemistry activity.

- Never taste, touch, or breathe in a chemical unless an adult tells you that you may.

1

Gemstones (above) are a solid, milk (right) is a liquid, and bubbles (next page) contain a gas.

Classifying Chemicals

When you're baking a cake, it is important to be able to describe and classify the ingredients. For example, a recipe might ask you to combine all of the dry ingredients and then mix them into the wet ingredients. So you would know to mix the dry flour and baking powder together before adding them to the wet oil, milk, and eggs. Chemists describe and classify chemicals in a similar way.

Solid, Liquid, or Gas?

What do oil, milk, and raw eggs have in common? They are all liquids. A liquid can flow and take the shape of the container that it is in.

By contrast, when you place an ice cube in a glass, the ice does not change its shape. It remains a cube (at least, until it melts). That's because ice is a solid. A solid keeps its shape no matter what container it is in.

If you use a straw to blow bubbles in a glass of milk, you will see another form that chemicals can take— a gas. The air inside of the milk bubbles is a gas. A gas expands to fill the entire container that it is in.

Activity

Temperature and Water Flow

In this activity, you will observe how the temperature of a liquid affects how the liquid flows.

1. Fill a **bowl** halfway with **cold water**.

2. Using a **toothpick**, poke a small hole in the side of a **foam cup** about a half inch from its base.

3. While holding your finger over the hole, fill the foam cup with **warm water**.

4. Add **food coloring** to the warm water in the foam cup.

5. Hold the foam cup in the bowl so that the water in the cup is just above the water in the bowl. Remove your finger from the hole.

6. Notice that the colored, warm water flows upward out of the cup's hole. It goes toward the top of the cold water in the bowl. How do you think temperature of the water affects the way the water flows?

7. Cold water sinks in hot water. How could you make an underwater fountain in which the colored water sinks after it exits the hole?

Chemists and other scientists conduct experiments to try to solve problems or answer questions. To do this, they follow the scientific method. First, they study and observe the things they have questions about. Next, they form a guess, called a hypothesis (hi PAH the sis), about what the answers might be. Then, they test the hypothesis with experiments. Finally, they analyze the test results and determine whether the results support the hypothesis, or if the hypothesis needs to be changed slightly or is completely wrong.

Density

The **density** of an object determines how much it weighs. When you place a solid object into a liquid, the object will either float to the top or sink to the bottom. If an object is less dense than water, it will float in water. If it is more dense, it will sink.

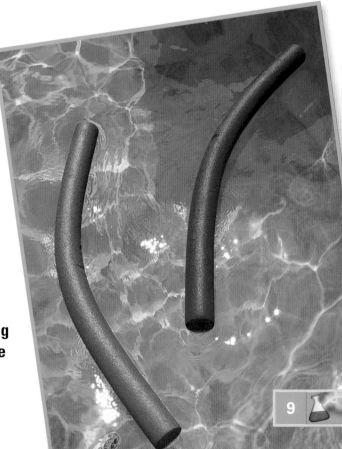

Do you think these swimming floats are less dense or more dense than water?

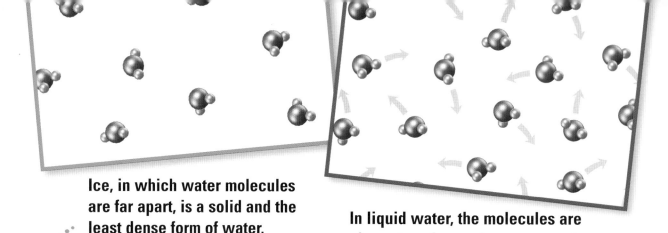

Ice, in which water molecules are far apart, is a solid and the least dense form of water.

In liquid water, the molecules are closer together and move around.

Activity

The Density of Water

In this activity, you will explore the densities of fresh water, salt water, and an egg.

1. Fill a **clear plastic cup** with **water**.

2. Gently place an **egg** in the water. Notice that the egg sinks. Which is less dense: fresh water or an egg?

3. Using a **spoon**, carefully remove the egg from the water.

In water vapor, a gas and the most dense form of water molecules are very close and bump into each other.

4. Add **two spoonfuls of salt** to the water and stir.

5. Gently place the egg in the salt water. Notice that the egg floats. Which is less dense: salt water or an egg? salt water or fresh water?

Seawater is salty, and lake water is not salty. Do you think that an egg will float in seawater or lake water?

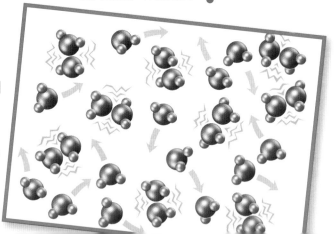

Activity

Float or Sink Challenge

In this activity, you will compare the densities of various objects in different liquids, which also have different densities.

1. Fill one-fourth of a **clear plastic cup** with **water**.

2. Fill one-fourth of a **second clear plastic cup** with **vegetable oil**.

3. Fill one-fourth of a **third clear plastice cup** with **rubbing alcohol**.

4. Choose **several solid objects**, **such as a paper clip**, **a birthday candle**, **a cork**, **a toothpick**, **a small plastic brick**, and **a marble**.

5. Find out which objects will float and which will sink by placing them in each liquid.

6. Try to layer the three liquids in a **fourth clear plastic cup** as shown below. Pour the liquids very carefully!

7. Find four objects, one that will float on each layer and a fourth that will sink to the bottom of the cup. Which of the three liquids is the least dense?

Cork

Rubbing Alcohol

Candle

Vegetable Oil

Plastic Brick

Water

Paper Clip

In this chapter, you learned that chemists classify chemicals as liquids, solids, or gases, based, in part, on the way they act when placed in a container. Liquids take the shape of a container, a solid keeps its own shape, and a gas expands to fill the container.

Density determines how much something weighs. You can tell the density of an object by watching how it acts in a liquid. Objects that float in a particular liquid are less dense than objects that sink.

Thought Challenges

- Can you name a solid, liquid, and gas in the picture of a glass of soda at left?

- A block of plastic weighs less than a block of iron that is the same size. Which is denser?

SIDETRIP ▶▶▶

Argonne National Laboratory is a research center near Chicago that is part of the United States Department of Energy. The chemists there perform a variety of research, including developing new drugs and adhesives (glues) and finding better ways to dispose of toxic waste.

- Steel is denser than water, and water is denser than wood. What will happen when you drop a piece of wood and piece of steel in a tub of water?

- Seawater is denser than oil. When a boat carrying oil crashes, the oil pours out into the ocean. Does the oil float on the surface or sink to the bottom of the ocean?

2

You can make different mixtures of homemade lemonade with a strong, medium, or weak flavor.

Mixing Chemicals Together

When you make instant pink lemonade, you add a scoop of powder to a glass of water and stir. It may seem like the powder has disappeared, but you can tell that it is still in the glass because the water is now pink and has a sweet taste. You made a **mixture** of the pink powder and the water. Chemists use mixtures all the time.

When you add too much powder to your lemonade mixture, the lemonade is very strong and tastes too sweet. It is more **concentrated** than you would like it to be. The concentration of a mixture refers to how much of a particular ingredient it contains. If you add too much water to the usual recipe, the resulting lemonade is weaker, or more **diluted,** than it should be. It will probably taste too bland to you.

Chemical Reactions

Sometimes when you mix chemicals together you get more

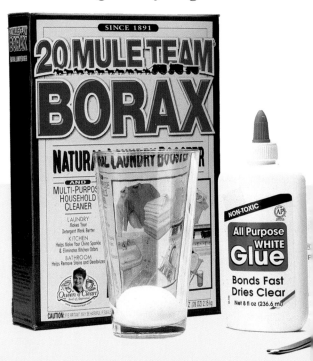

Activity

How Do You Make Glop?
In this activity, you will use a chemical reaction to make a rubbery chemical.

1. In a *small plastic cup,* mix *two spoonfuls of white glue* with *four spoonfuls of water.*

2. In a *second plastic cup,* mix *half a spoonful of powdered borax* with *three-fourths cup of water.*

3. Add two spoonfuls of the borax mixture to the cup with the glue mixture.

than a mixture—you get a brand new chemical. For example, when you add vinegar to baking soda, bubbles of a gas start to form. The gas is **carbon dioxide**. When chemicals change to form new chemicals, a **chemical reaction** is taking place.

4. Stir and then allow the glop to sit for one minute. A chemical reaction takes place when you add the borax to the glue. The new chemical that forms is completely different from the original ingredients.

5. Form the glop into a shape, such as a cube or a ball. Does it keep its shape? How does it feel? What do you think would happen if you added more water or glue than recommended?

Useful Chemical Reactions

There are many chemical reactions that are useful to people every day. For example, a chemical reaction in cake batter causes gases to be released, giving a baked cake a spongy texture.

Without a chemical reaction, this cake would not be so fluffy.

 **Activity**

Cupcake Batter Challenge

In this activity, you will explore how changing the amount of chemicals affects a chemical reaction in cupcake batter.

1. Label **five plain paper cups** one through five.

2. In a **small bowl**, mix together **six tablespoons of flour** and **four tablespoons of sugar**.

3. Put two tablespoons of the flour–and–sugar mixture into each of the labeled cups.

4. Add **baking soda** to the paper cups according to the following chart. Then mix the ingredients.

Cup	Amount of Baking Soda
1	none
2	1/8 teaspoon
3	1/4 teaspoon
4	1/2 teaspoon
5	1 teaspoon

5. In the empty bowl, mix **five tablespoons of water** with **one tablespoon of vinegar** and **one-fourth teaspoon of vanilla**.

Unwanted Reactions

Some chemical reactions are not useful. For example, a chemical reaction between iron particles and oxygen in the air causes some metal objects to rust.

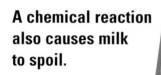

A chemical reaction also causes milk to spoil.

6. Add **one tablespoon of vegetable oil** and one tablespoon of the water, vinegar, and vanilla mixture to each labeled cup. Stir all five batters until they are smooth.

7. Place the cups on a **plate** in a **microwave oven** and cook for three minutes, rotating them at least once.

8. Remove the cups from the microwave oven and allow the cupcakes to cool for five minutes.

9. Carefully remove the cupcakes from the cups and compare them. Which cupcake is the tallest? Are some cupcakes spongier than others? How does the amount of baking soda added to the batter affect the cupcakes? You'll find that the more baking soda you add, the taller and spongier the cupcake will be. Why do you think this is so?

The reaction that causes rust is called **oxidation**. Rusty metal is often weak and can cause damage to buildings, cars, and boats. To prevent rusting, you can paint a metal object so that it is protected from the air.

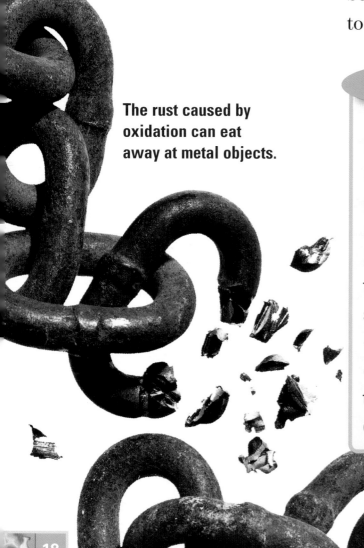

The rust caused by oxidation can eat away at metal objects.

In this chapter, you learned that the concentration of a chemical mixture is determined by how much of a particular ingredient it contains. A chemical reaction takes place when chemicals change to form new materials. Some of the reactions are useful to us, and others are undesirable.

on the job

Some chemists work for private companies, others work for the government, and still others work at universities or other schools. Many chemists perform research to design everyday products, such as shampoos, toothpaste, cleaners, and medicines. Other chemists perform pure research that advances the understanding of science.

Thought Challenges

- When you mix sugar and water, the mixture looks exactly like plain water. How do you know that it is really a mixture and not pure water?

- Your father makes two one-gallon batches of a fruit drink using a powdered mix. One batch is darker than the other. Which batch contains more of the drink mix?

- You add three spoonfuls of salt to a cup of water and two spoonfuls of salt to a second cup of water. Which mixture is more concentrated?

- You leave a shiny copper pot outside for several months. You notice that it is now dull and green. The green color does not come from green paint. How else can you explain the color change?

Did You Know ?

A chemical reaction between copper and air causes copper statues to turn green. The Statue of Liberty is green because a layer of a green chemical has formed on its copper surface.

- Give an example of a useful chemical reaction that can become an unwanted chemical reaction.

Many cleaning products contain bases, while citrus fruits, such as oranges, contain acids.

Acids and Bases

Scientists try to classify chemicals into categories of substances that resemble each other in some way. This helps them understand chemicals better. Two common categories are **acids** and **bases**.

Acids

Grapefruit juice and lemon juice are both sour. Sometimes orange juice that has not been sweetened is also sour. All three of these juices come from citrus fruits. Citrus fruits are sour because they contain a type of chemical called an acid.

Citrus fruits and many other foods have small amounts of safe acids. However, other substances have harmful acids, such as the sulfuric acid in car batteries. Sulfuric acid can burn your skin.

Bases

If you have ever gotten soap in your mouth when you were washing your face, you may have noticed that it was bitter. The bitter taste comes partly from a chemical called a base. Many bases are harmful if swallowed, though others are used to make foods. Ammonia, detergents, and baking soda contain bases. Never taste a chemical to determine if it is an acid or base!

Activity

Secret Writing

In this activity, you will see how bases cause certain chemical reactions.

1. Sprinkle a small amount of **powdered dish detergent** in a **paper cup** .

Can you see how the litmus paper shows that vinegar (left) is an acid, and ammonia (next page) is a base?

2. Add **two spoonfuls of water** and stir.

3. Using the detergent and water mixture as ink, take a **small paintbrush** and write a message on a sheet of **notebook paper** .

4. Allow the message to dry.

5. Rinse the brush thoroughly. After rinsing, sprinkle a small amount of **tumeric**

Activity

How Can You Find Acids and Bases?

In this activity, you will make test strips that can identify acids and bases.

1. Place *half a cup of shredded purple cabbage leaves* into a *foam cup.* Fill with *hot water.*

2. Allow the water to cool at least fifteen minutes.

3. Using a *spoon,* remove all of the leaves from the water and throw them away. Save the cabbage water.

(a food flavoring) in a **second paper cup**.

6. Add **two spoonfuls of rubbing alcohol** to the cup and stir.

7. To make the secret message appear, brush the turmeric–and–alcohol mixture over the message. You should be able to read the message because the base detergent causes turmeric to change color.

IDs for Acids and Bases

Chemicals can be identified as acids or bases by looking for a color change when they are mixed with other chemicals. Chemists use paper called **litmus paper,** which turns pink in acids and blue in bases, to help them identify certain chemicals.

4. Cut up a *coffee filter* into several strips, each about the size of your finger. Soak the strips in the cabbage water.

5. Spread the wet strips out onto a sheet of *wax paper.* Allow them to dry overnight.

6. Use these strips to test *various liquids, such as club soda, apple juice, and vinegar.* The strips will turn from pale blue to pale green when dipped in a base, and pale blue to pale pink when dipped in an acid.

Neutral Chemicals

Many chemicals are neither acids nor bases. These chemicals are neutral. Water is a neutral chemical. If you put a litmus paper strip in water, there will be no color change.

Acids and bases can be mixed together to make a neutral mixture. For example, your stomach makes an acid called hydrochloric acid. It is used to help break down the food that you eat. When your stomach makes too much acid, you can get painful heartburn. An antacid tablet contains a base that mixes with the stomach acid in a chemical reaction. The chemicals that form from this reaction are neutral and do not cause any pain.

Activity

Polishing Pennies Challenge

In this activity, you will compare what you know about acids and bases to determine which will polish a dull penny best.

1. Collect **ten pennies that are not shiny**. Be sure that they are all similar in color.

2. Design a test to find the best way to polish a penny. Pick **ten liquids** to test. **For example you may want to try dish soap, vinegar, or even hot sauce**.

3. Which liquid polished a penny the best? Compare your results with a friend.

4. Test each liquid with **litmus paper** to see if it is an acid or a base. You should find that acids polish pennies best because they remove a dull substance that forms when the copper of a penny contacts air.

Heartburn is a burning feeling in your chest caused by an acid.

In this chapter, you learned that some products, such as vinegar, are sour and contain a chemical called an acid. Products with a bitter taste, such as detergent, contain a chemical called a base. You can identify if a chemical is an acid or a base by using litmus paper. Chemicals that are neither acids nor bases are neutral.

Thought Challenges

- Why do you think chewable vitamin C tablets might taste sour?

- Coffee is an acid, though it tastes very bitter like a base. What is a safe way to show that coffee is an acid?

- A cleaning product contains ammonia, a base. What color would the cleaning product turn purple cabbage strips?

- Would you add an acid or a base to lemon juice to make a neutral mixture?

Conclusion

If you tried any of the activities in this book, you're now a beginning chemist. Congratulations! Experimenting with or reading about these activities may help you remember several important ideas that chemists work with.

One of the most basic things that chemists need to know in their work is whether chemical materials are solids, liquids, or gases. They often conduct experiments in which a material may change from one of these forms to another.

In other experiments, chemists may observe whether an object sinks or floats in a liquid. Such observations tell a chemist about the object's density. This type of information is often valuable in determining what materials are made of and what they may be used for.

Chemists make mixtures of different concentrations all the time in their experiments. In many of these mixtures, chemical reactions happen, causing major changes in the chemicals. Such changes sometimes lead to the creation of brand new, useful substances. For example, much of the food we eat, the clothes we wear, and the other things we use came from chemical reactions produced by chemists.

Many opportunities to question and explore ideas like a chemist are all around us every day. Chemistry is as close as our kitchens!

Glossary

acids chemicals that taste sour and turn litmus paper pink

bases chemicals that taste bitter and turn litmus paper blue

carbon dioxide gas that is part of the atmosphere and that is produced in certain chemical reactions

chemical reaction change in chemicals that happens when they are mixed together

chemists scientists who explore different kinds of chemicals and what they do

chemistry study of what everything is made of

concentrated when a mixture has more than the normal amount of a particular ingredient in it

density measurement of how much material makes up an object

diluted when a mixture has less than the normal amount of a particular ingredient in it

litmus paper special paper that turns pink in acids and blue in bases

mixture combination of different substances

oxidation combination of oxygen with another chemical to form a new substance

Index